"I absolutely love this book. Reading it felt like spending time with a trusted friend. Its tone is supportive and it's full of suggestions for small changes that can make a big difference in our lives. I recommend this book to joyful, old dames everywhere."

Wendy Leeds, LCSW and author of <u>Calm and Sense</u>

"Eating healthy, exercising, getting an adequate amount of sleep and social connection are all crucial to creating a healthy microbiome and living a long fulfilling life! Giving your body the nutrients it needs and creating meaningful relationships with peers, coworkers and/or loved ones can boost the immune system and fend off diseases. The 5 pillars are a great system to incorporate into your daily life to promote longevity."

Katie Gaughan, BSN, Elder Care Specialty

"An easy read, clear, concise and fun steps to attain your goals. Peg is a wonderful role model and mentor for life long wellness. ~~Skinny~~ Joyful Old Dame is a great addition and follow-up to her earlier book Food Becomes You."

Joanne Walsh RN

"With this handy pocket-sized guide by your side, you'll say 'See you later!' to toxic diet culture and 'Hello!' to a life that leaves you mentally and physically fulfilled. By following Peg's Five Pillars of Lifelong Wellness, you can learn to sustain your health and find true happiness in your later years. You only live once, so make it count!"

Katie Duval – Executive Director, Medfield TV

"I finished your book!!!!!! Loved it!!!! Short but sweet without being sugar coated. Loved that I could read it and digest it (without the calories) quickly. Simple and to the point with no fluff!!!

"I want to buy it for Christmas and give it to my female friends. I'll put my order in now for at least 25 copies!!!!

"You are amazing!!"

Patti Giuliano, DC, author of Holy Sh*t, I'm Going to Be a Mom

"No truer words have been spoken, Health is your greatest Wealth! Spot on!

"My French Chef Mentors all taught me one important lesson about Food and Life. 'Surtout faites simples', meaning, Above all, keep it simple.

"My mother told me 'I had ants in my pants' so for self-help and self-maintenance, I like a book that lays it out like an episode of Dragnet..... Just the facts, ma'am. Your book has given us the template that feeds our desire to acquire longevity with a smile."

Andrew Wilkinson, Executive Chef

"For many years Peg has been my beacon as I aspire to live a healthy life. Many guides and books focus on identifying where things have gone wrong and correcting faults, but Peg's approach is consistently the opposite because she firmly believes in finding the joy in everyday living. Joyful Old Dame should remind every one of us that it is never too late to make a fresh start, connect with others, look at life through a new lens, and realize we likely possess the necessary tools to thrive."

Mary Beth Shertick, Research Administrator

"Often when I help clients plan for retirement, medical expenses that could have been avoided with better habits end up being one of their largest expenses and not for the faint of heart. People need to invest in themselves to experience healthy aging. Healthy clients get to invest in hiking trips in Europe, a yoga membership, a bicycle, or visiting friends in different parts of the world. Staying active and feeling good is very rewarding and a much better way to spend your hard earned savings."

Robert L. Benoit, CFP®, Compass Investment Group

"There are so many tips in this gem of a book. The 5 pillars guide you along the path toward easy choices and clear thinking. Peg has synthesized years of training, education and client mentoring into a readable book that you will enjoy as a resource in your health journey. This book will help you as it has helped me, no matter your age. Enjoy."

Rebecca Stephenson Medical Writer, Board Certified Women's Health Physical Therapist

~~Skinny~~ Joyful Old Dame

Peg Doyle

All efforts have been made to ensure the accuracy of the information contained in this book as of the date published. The author and the publisher expressly disclaim responsibility for any adverse effects arising from the use or application of the information contained herein.

© 2024 Peg Doyle, M.Ed., CHHC. All rights reserved.

~~Skinny~~ Joyful Old Dame
ISBN: 979-8-9918538-0-4 paperback

Cover design and illustrations by the talented Angi Shearstone

No part of this book may be used or reproduced in any manner whatsoever without written permission except for brief quotations embedded in critical articles and reviews. For information contact Peg Doyle at wellnessandyou.com . The scanning, uploading and distribution of this book by the Internet or any other means without the permission of the author is illegal.

Please purchase only authorized print or electronic versions of the book. Copyright 2024. Morning Sun Women.

Printed in the United States.
Address is 41 Philip St., Medfield, MA 02052
or peg@wellnessandyou.com

Acknowledgements

This book is dedicated to all the dames who have struggled to be perfect.

My hope is that the tools you find here will show you that dieting and deprivation are distractions from the real keys to your happiness and well being. It's time to be joyful!

Joyfulness is indeed found in self-care and the acknowledgement that you have always been perfect, just the way you are.

Fall in love with the beautiful gift that is your life, and live it to the fullest.

Contents

INTRODUCTION i

A Bowl of Goodness 2

Movement Should Be Fun 4

There's Nothing Like a Good Night's Sleep 6

Shake It Off 8

Friends are Lasting Treasures 10

Put the Pieces Together 12

Notes on My Becoming 17

a note from peg 18

About the Author 19

INTRODUCTION
Into the Rapids

"Aging is out of your control; how you handle it though, is in your hands."
Diane Von Furstenberg

Okay ladies, right off the top we're going to dispense with the skinny adjective. Since my early 50s I've been a health coach for thousands of women. I've seen your struggles and shared some of them, most of which I attribute to this: pressure from the diet and beauty industries to lose weight; being told by your doctor to lose weight; being told by your own self to lose weight; and being inundated by ads from the food industry making processed foods irresistible.

There are better things you can do with your life than count points or drink meals.

It is liberating to kiss those miserable dieting days good-bye and recognize that women's wellness is a loftier way to spend your time. Adios to calorie counting and deprivation, pills and side effects.

Getting to the heart of self care will help you with your weight more than any diet can.

This little book is not only for those of us who define ourselves as older, but also for women in their fifties who may have struggled for years and now just want to get healthy. Know that aging is not a disease. This little book provides the tools for lasting health.

We're old enough to know by now that a size 6 may be far less important than an intact body that functions well. Besides, we need to put our energy into being joyful and well so we can experience healthy aging without dieting.

I don't ask the women I coach to weigh themselves every day, or every week, for that matter. What I do ask them is to eat real food and to cook it themselves as much as they can. I ask them to look at what brings them joy in life and to get more of it. I ask them to get a good night's sleep. I ask them to make time for fun. To summarize, I ask them to love themselves.

As Maya Angelou said "You alone are enough. You have nothing to prove to anybody."

So as you're going into, or are midstream in what some call our Third Phase or the Wisdom Years, let go of perfection. Let go of outsiders idea of who you should be and how you should look. And get comfortable with being older and wiser. Seek out senior women lifestyle tips that will give you a clear path to longevity. Wear your years with pride. <u>Care less about the scale so you can care more about your authentic self.</u> It will free you up to really love yourself as a Joyful Old Dame. It's time for you to practice extreme self care. You've earned it!

One Wise Woman

When I was a young 40 something I vacationed with friends on the beautiful island of Turks and Caicos in the British Virgin Isles. One day we ventured out of the resort and found our way into the village, had a cappuccino, and as we ambled back to the resort an island lady stopped and offered us a ride. We hopped in and as we chatted about how much we loved the island and its resident dolphin JoJo, she offered that she was on her way to her weekly luncheon with other island ladies and invited us to join them. We jumped at the chance.

~~Skinny~~ Joyful Old Dame

When we got there I was randomly seated beside a lovely lady named Charlotte. She told me she and her husband lived on the island for 15 years, was recently widowed, and just sold her villa. I asked her what's next for her. She replied, "I ordered an RV and will pick it up in Miami. Then I will drive cross country, up into Canada where I'll settle near my son and his family." Never having traveled alone in my life I said "My, that seems like a really ambitious and brave thing to do." She replied "Well, I'm 81 years old, I'm in the rapids now, I have no time to waste."

Charlotte's words have stayed with me ever since that breezy afternoon luncheon on the Island. All these years later I realize I'm in the rapids now; I have no time to waste.

Most of you who pick up this book are in the rapids, or edging toward them. So grab your paddle and let's figure out how to enjoy the ride.

These next pages will give you the scoop on how to be a vibrant Joyful Old Dame. It's a formula I call the Five Pillars of Lifelong Wellness. You'll find five sections, each one listing the keys to success in each category. Come along for the ride. Join me! You'll be glad you did.

Peg Doyle

~~Skinny~~ Joyful Old Dame

Ten steps. Your longevity roadmap. No dieting. Life changing.

Skinny Joyful Old Dame

A Bowl of Goodness

Chapter 1   Pillar One
Nutrition

"I know that once people get connected to real food, they never change back"
Alice Waters, American restaurateur, chef, and food activist

We all need reminders when it comes to eating healthy, no matter how knowledgeable we are or how new we are to understanding the power of nutrition.

Remember, food should be enjoyed, not feared. The following items will lead you to a healthy relationship with food. Make changes slowly and they are sure to stick.

Make It Real Food for Real Happiness

- notice when you are hungry and sit down for meals
- notice when you are full; you can do this when you eat consciously and slowly
- nourish yourself with whole foods
- avoid processed foods; they are filled with chemicals
- cook more at home; you will know what you are eating
- eat less meat, more veggies, grains, beans, fruit, nuts and seeds
- eat meals; they will keep you from grazing on empty calories
- don't aim for perfection; leave space for small pleasures
- drink more water, especially on awakening and 1/2 hour before meals
- quit night eating

Ten steps. Your longevity roadmap. No dieting. Life changing.

~~Skinny~~ *Joyful Old Dame*

Movement Should Be Fun

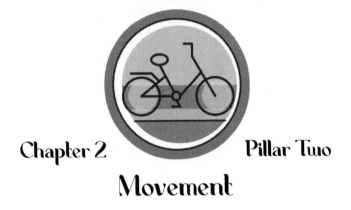

Chapter 2 — Pillar Two
Movement

"I want to keep going and do what I want to do"
World traveler Kay Willoughby

Humans are made for movement. When we choose an activity we love, movement becomes pure pleasure. Care for your body so it is ready for playtime.

- connect with Nature; it's good medicine
- focus on balance and strength
- crawl if you can for neurological stimulation
- stretch upon awakening and before bedtime
- choose a movement you like; sport, workout, dancing, yoga, walking, etc.
- carve out time at least 3 days a week for active movement
- mix up your activities so you use all your muscles, including your brain
- wear comfortable shoes that support your feet and your balance
- massage your feet every day to keep them limber
- get regular bodywork like shiatsu, acupuncture, massage or chiropractic to identify and correct any misalignments

Ten steps. Your longevity roadmap. No dieting. Life changing.

Skinny Joyful Old Dame

There's Nothing Like a Good Night's Sleep

Chapter 3 — **Pillar Three**

Sleep

"Without enough sleep, we all become tall two year olds."
– JoJo Jensen, American Voice Talent

Sleep is the time your mind and your body shed unwanted debris and generate healthy cells. Your last meal should be fully digested before you lie down. Experiment with some of these non-medicinal techniques that help you wind down well before you get into bed. Find a sleep schedule that works for you and stick to it.

Create your own Lullaby

- wind down from the day
- lower the lights after dinner
- let early dinner be your last food before sleep
- remember sleep is your body's repair time
- turn off tech an hour before bedtime
- take a warm bath or shower
- massage your body
- use aromatherapy such as dried lavender, sandalwood or ylang-ylang
- cool down your bedroom for better sleep
- choose the mattress, pillow and bed linens that are right for you

Ten steps. Your longevity roadmap. No dieting. Life changing.

~~Skinny~~ Joyful Old Dame

Shake It Off

Chapter 4   Pillar Four

Manage Stress

"It's not about how fast you run or how high you climb but how well you bounce."
Vivian Komori, CEO of the Broad Perspective

Fifty percent of all doctor's office visits are for stress-related ailments and complaints. Become aware of how stress affects you. Identify actions you can take to ease your stress.

Let it go

- build resilience by keeping your mind open to options
- breathe from your belly, slow and steady
- meditate or pray daily, not just when you are overwhelmed
- identify what you cannot control and stop trying to manage it
- create a daily practice of writing down what you are grateful for
- stay with your routines; they are grounding
- notice and replace negative thoughts with positive thoughts
- don't isolate when you are stressed
- limit exposure to media that highlights fear or tragedy
- use your favorite music to relax; music soothes the soul

Ten steps. Your longevity roadmap. No dieting. Life changing.

~~Skinny~~ *Joyful Old Dame*

Friends are Lasting Treasures

Chapter 5 **Pillar Five**

Social Connection

"I can promise you that women working together — linked, informed, and educated — can bring peace and prosperity to this forsaken planet."

– Isabel Allende, is a Chilean-American writer

Social connection is the glue that keeps us going, in good times and bad. Make friendships a priority for your health and well-being.

We are one

- be your authentic self and you'll attract kindred spirits
- be vulnerable with trusted friends
- listen more than you speak
- share your heart and your energy
- practice kindness - it is good medicine
- reach out and extend a helping hand
- ask for help when you need it - we all will one day
- organize or participate in social gatherings
- smile - it's contagious
- hug - it can literally save a life

Ten steps. Your longevity roadmap. No dieting. Life changing.

~~Skinny~~ Joyful Old Dame

Put the Pieces Together

Chapter 6

"Beauty is the beginning and end of fulfillment. Beauty resides within us. She is the divine, human heart."
— Dana Hutton, Author

None of the Five Pillars stands alone. Yet when they all stand tall, you have all the tools you need to truly be well and vital. You will see that longevity is not just about years, but it is also about your ability to add life to those years. When you embrace these 5 Pillars you give yourself the tools to support your longevity.

You can strengthen your pillars by starting with one or two items from each pillar. Build these items into your daily routine. Keep building and make note of how the actions you are taking impact your sense of joy.

And finally, in my opinion, the Pillar that most visibly makes us Joyful Old Dames is Social Connection. Oh, do we need each other! Whether living alone, with a partner or with a host of others, there's nothing quite like a connection with other women. It doesn't matter the age since we now understand that it's the connection that matters. A time for listening, speaking, laughing, crying, helping and learning. Social connection is a platform for creativity, vitality and happiness.

In this post-pandemic era, we are still coming out of our shells. Shells that protected us from the known and the unknown, and sadly, shells that isolated us for a very long time. Your social connection muscle may still feel a little rusty. The only way to get it strong again is to oil it with practice.

Imagine the ripple effect of your phone call, your invitation, your outreach, not only for you but for those whose lives you touch.

Joyful Old Dames are meant to connect.

The Never Ending Art of *BECOMING More*

A funny thing happens when you fully embrace the 5 Pillars. Your mind is clearer. You know yourself better. You may ask yourself, "What now?" You're in a great place, ready for new adventures.

Luckily you have at least two living generations of women to look at as examples of Joyful Old Dames who live life to the fullest. These are women who paid little or no attention to their age or their weight or dress size and kept growing and contributing in some way to their own lives and might also have influenced yours.

In celebrity circles women like Meryl Streep, Gloria Steinem and Diane von Furstenberg come to mind. These Dames are in their 70s and 80s and give little time to worrying about their weight or being perfect. They have more important things to focus on. There's an urgency around things that matter to them. They are constantly *BECOMING* more, deepening their imprint and impact on the world around them.

In your own life, you may have women who impressed you by their passion for life, their constant *BECOMING*. They may have a goal they are focused on or simply a joyful way of looking at life that is truly contagious. Can you think of women like that? I'm lucky enough to know a few.

Edith is a woman in her mid 80s who is an active advocate for the environment. She was injured by pesticides and to prevent harm to others she is a vocal advocate for regulation. Ann, at age 90, is a former member of town governance and although legally blind, uses her social media platform to keep connected with town residents. Joan, age 93 is a former dancer and livens up her water aerobics class with her wit and vitality. Magda, a talented artist at age 91, lights up at the mere thought of getting into her studio. At 85, Helen is delighted each time a quilting weekend is scheduled with her friends.

These women don't have time for the distractions of dieting or needing to be perfect. Using the 5 Pillars is a more effective way to remain vital and excited about life. These women are engaged in the art of constantly *BECOMING* more of their whole selves.

An Exercise for You

Would you agree that you do your best when you have a plan? With a plan you will be able to envision and execute a lifetime of constantly *BECOMING*. There is no end to your growth and engagement when *you* have your plan for *BECOMING*. And there's no place to doubt yourself by suggesting you are 'too old'.

Take some time to look back, look at the present, and look at the future you envision. Make a list of the key moments of your past and present that shaped you into the woman you are today. You may find that your past led you to *BECOME* who you are today.

Then envision your future self in your Third Chapter or Wisdom Years. Get excited. Get inspired and committed to having the best years ahead of you.

After all, you are *BECOMING* a *JOYFUL OLD DAME*.

Notes on My Becoming

a note from peg

Dear Reader,

A huge thank you for choosing to read this little book ~~Skinny~~ Joyful Old Dame.

If you enjoyed it and want to learn more about vital living, visit my website <u>wellnessandyou.com</u> where you will find a wealth of information on nutrition and lifestyle and an opportunity for a free subscription to my Wellness and You newsletter.

You are also invited to join my online Facebook community of women called Joyful Old Dames. This site will be an instant link to like-minded women and future opportunities to engage in virtual and live events.

I am available to speak to your organization and spread the word about the unlimited possibilities of becoming a Joyful Old Dame. Life is to be enjoyed from start to finish and when you have the tools to make your last chapters joyful ones, you will be glad you lived to a fine old age.

With love,

Peg

About the Author

Peg Doyle, M.Ed., CHHC is deeply passionate about helping women uncover their potential. She is an advocate for releasing oneself from the confines of dieting and weight obsession, replacing these limitations with a holistic focus on overall wellbeing.

Trained in Eastern bodywork and holistic health counseling, Peg received a postgraduate certificate in Gerontology from the renowned McCormack Center at University of Massachusetts and a certificate in Behavioral Change from Yale University. She integrates these diverse approaches to celebrate the uniqueness of every woman.

Her work inspires women to embrace their true selves and to thrive at every stage of life.

Skinny Joyful Old Dame
_____

Made in the USA
Middletown, DE
10 January 2025